The Reiki Symbol Masterclass:

Unconventional Approaches to Symbol Mastery

by Taggart King

www.reiki-evolution.co.uk

taggart@reiki-evolution.co.uk

Contents

About This Masterclass

This manual and workbook is all about working with symbols but it is not a standard Reiki book and you will be learning things here that really are not taught anywhere in the world of Reiki, as far as I can tell.

You are going to be hearing things that may well contradict what you were taught, but all I ask that you keep an open mind and just bear with me, and use the exercises in this workbook to prove to your own satisfaction that what I am saying is correct.

This book is full of Reiki heresies!

I am going to give you the opportunity to experience the energies that symbols elicit, and you will be doing this in a variety of ways.

You will start by using traditional Reiki symbols (but probably in a different way than you are used to, if you didn't train with Reiki Evolution) and then you will move on to explore the energies created or represented by other symbols or graphical representations.

None of these other symbols will you have been "attuned" to!

You will discover for yourself that you do not need to have been "attuned" to a symbol for it to work for you.

You will discover that each symbol produces a characteristic energy.

And, as an aside, that also means that if you are going to work with the Reiki symbols, you need to be working with the right ones, not ones that have morphed and changed or been deliberately altered

6

along the way… because you will not be eliciting what was originally intended by the founder of our system.

And once your energy-perceiving muscles have been flexed and developed a bit, we will move on to learn a system I developed where you can use your intuition to create bespoke symbols for yourself and to help other people, and to create symbols for particular purposes.

This is a complete, detailed and deep course in Reiki energetics, so strap yourself in because we are in for a bit of a ride!

You have some work to do. ☺

Background

For the purpose of this course, when I talk about a "symbol" I am going to refer to any 2D shape that can be drawn or brushed or designed on paper and looked at.

Symbols can be in black and white or colour, they can be simple or detailed, they can originate with some esoteric tradition or practice or they can be entirely novel, made up, or channelled.

Reiki, certainly in the way that it is usually taught in the West, in lineages that derive from Dr Hayashi and Mrs Takata, uses symbols, which are shapes or Japanese characters.

There are three symbols taught at Second Degree and one at Master/Teacher level.

The original symbols have mutated and distorted to a greater or lesser degree in different lineages, as they were passed from teacher to student, teacher to student.

In some lineages the symbols have been deliberately changed, being taught as a mirror image of the original, or both versions (original and mirror image) being taught together.

Other symbols have crept into Reiki from various sources and there are many Reiki variations being taught, each with its own set of additional symbols that had nothing to do with what Mikao Usui was teaching.

Symbols in Usui's time

Now, it may surprise you to discover that symbols did not feature at all as far as the vast majority of Mikao Usui's students were concerned. Not only that, but Usui Sensei did not use attunements, did not attune anyone to anything and his system wasn't really about treating people.

I think I need to unpack this a bit…

What Usui was teaching was basically a personal or spiritual development system, with the ability to treat other people seen as an interesting side-effect of the main thrust of his teachings. Students did some simple energy exercises, embraced mindfulness, and lived their lives according to Usui's precepts.

As they continued to work with Usui, students were introduced to various energies and states and almost all his students used either Buddhist-style meditations or chanted Shinto mantras to elicit and experience these energies/states.

So, where do the symbols fit in?

Well, Usui Sensei taught symbols to the Imperial Officers predoinantly, people who had approached him asking to be taught a hands-on healing system that they intended to use and have used in the Imperial Navy.

Usui taught them symbols to use in this context, and one or two of his other students were taught symbols too, so that they could use them to elicit energies that the majority of students were using meditations and chanting to elicit.

Bespoke training

Usui Sensei varied what he taught according to the needs of the individual, so there was not a "one size fits all" approach: Shinto followers chanted Shinto mantras, Buddhists used Buddhist-style meditations initially, and a very, very few people got symbols.

So the Reiki that is taught in the West is not really representative of what Usui Sensei was doing and teaching.

Usui Sensei and "attunements"

In the West we have "attunements", don't we, and there is this idea that an attunement "attunes" you to a symbol (often with the notion that to practise Reiki you have to be attuned to certain symbols, and if you have not been attuned to a symbol then it will not work properly or at all).

And there used to be this belief, which is less often encountered nowadays, that you had to have a certain specific number of attunements in order to have been attuned 'properly'.

Looking from the vantage point of Mikao Usui's original system, this seems a very strange state of affairs because Usui Sensei:

1. Did not use attunements
2. Did not teach attunements
3. Did not attune anyone to anything

Usui Sensei 'empowered' people with Reiki and he did not use a physical ritual: he empowered people using intent.

Where did attunements come from?

These were created after Usui Sensei's death by the Imperial Officers, who invented attunements as a way of recreating for themselves the experience that they had when receiving 'intent' empowerments from Mikao Usui, conveying this through a physical ritual.

And because they had been taught symbols by Usui, their attunement rituals involved the use of symbols. A symbol-using attunement ritual was passed on from Dr Hayashi to Mrs Takata, and then through various Western lineages, morphing and changing as it was passed from one teacher to another.

There is no one standard attunement ritual used in the world of Reiki, but endless different variations, some more complex, some less complex, some using techniques or practices and symbols from non-Reiki traditions.

In some lineages you need one attunement, in others you receive two or more. There is no consensus about what an attunement ritual should look like, other than that people tend to stick with what they were taught, or maybe tweak it a bit, or more than a bit, to suit their interests or worldviews.

So we have ended up with the situation where people believe that to be able to practise Reiki you have to be attuned, that you have to be attuned to particular symbols, and that it is only once you have been attuned to a symbol that it will work for you.

This is problematic because if you wind back a century then you see a system that does not use attunements and which hardly uses symbols, and when symbols are used, they are there to represent a particular aspect of the energy, and these symbols were used with no-one having been "attuned" to them.

And it is further complicated because they way that Reiki symbols are used in most lineages, when treating people, for example, is a world away from how they were used in Mikao Usui's original system.

Ideas of creating "symbol sandwiches", where you create a stack of symbols in a particular order for particular purposes, or the idea that you have to draw one of the Reiki symbols over other symbols to 'empower' them, has nothing to do with what Mikao Usui was teaching and is a very 'un-Japanese' way of approaching things.

In the original system, students used Shinto mantras, Buddhist-style meditations or, very occasionally, a symbol to represent two important energies that you had to embrace on your journey of spiritual development: earth ki and heavenly ki.

Treating others was a side-issue, not what the system was all about, and if it was done at all it was carried out in a very simple fashion.

And the idea of a "Power symbol" would have been a complete nonsense.

So, what do symbols do?

Symbols frame the energy in a particular way, they emphasise a particular aspect of what is there.

You could view them as creating or eliciting a particular "frequency", but I put that word in inverted commas because I think it is just a useful way of looking at things rather than an expression of reality or truth.

Another useful image to bring to mind to understand the use of symbols is that of a magnifying glass, where by narrowing the focus you actually make things more intense, and this is what happens when you focus your attention on a particular symbol, I believe: you narrow your focus and make things more intense as a result.

Any symbol will focus or frame or elicit a particular aspect or 'frequency' of the energy.

You already have 'all frequencies' available to you, so it is just a matter of degree and emphasis.

And whether you use one of Mikao Usui's original symbols, or a symbol from some different tradition, or channeled symbols, they will all frame the energy in a particular way without you having had to have been 'attuned' to them (whatever that means!).

Basic Practice

Energy work

To get the most out of this course, you need to be working with the energy regularly, you need to have a basic energy practice running in the background, and what I recommend is as follows, both practices forming part of the original system that Usui Sensei taught:

1. Kenyoku/Joshin Kokkyu ho*
2. Usui's Self-treatment meditation

* If you wish, you can use the full "Hatsurei ho" sequence

MP3 tracks that talk you through Hatsurei ho and Mikao Usui's Self-treatment meditation can be found on the Reiki Evolution web site.

Use this QR code to find them:

I recommend that you aim to carry out these exercises each day (or certainly most days: don't beat yourself up for not being perfect!). They provide a good, background practice, they cleanse and they balance, and they will give you a solid foundation to work from.

Mindfulness

You will also benefit if you start to explore the practice of mindfulness and introduce mindfulness into your daily routines, for example when you do the washing up or go for a walk or eat an orange, and I can recommend two books, both by Thich Nhat Hanh:

"The Miracle of Mindfulness"

"Peace is Every Step".

The Precepts

And finally, you will benefit from a regular pondering of Mikao Usui's precepts, considering how embracing them can change the way that you think, feel, behave and respond to people.

It was said that you could achieve as much spiritual development through following the precepts as you could through carrying out the energy work, so the precepts are not an interesting add-on, a side-issue: they are at the very centre of the system, as is mindfulness.

Mindfulness helps you to embody the precepts and the precepts put into words the benefits of being mindful in your daily life, and in your practice of Reiki.

The two intertwine and flow through each other, reflecting each other and enhancing each other.

What can be a very powerful approach with regard to the precepts is to use a technique that I created called "precepts rehearsal" and you can read about that in this blog.

Use this QR code to read the blog:

Experiencing Earth Ki & Heavenly Ki

So let's start with some symbols that you will be familiar with, two symbols that are taught at Second Degree: CKR and SHK (ChoKuRei and SeiHeKi).

In Western-style Reiki CKR is often referred to as "the power symbol" (which is an unfortunate misunderstanding) and SHK is often referred to as "the mental/emotional symbol".

And these symbols are often used in different combinations, as symbol "sandwiches" and the like, for various purposes, with CKR often being plonked on top of another symbol or symbols to 'empower' them.

This is an entirely un-Japanese approach, has nothing to do with the original system that Usui taught, so we won't be going there.

We keep things simple!

In the original system that Usui taught, students at Second Degree were introduced to two important energies that they meditated on either using Buddhist-style meditations or using Shinto mantras.

These two energies were that of earth ki and heavenly ki, two fundamental aspects of the energy, two fundamental aspects of who we are, and you can use CKR and SHK to elicit these energies.

CKR elicits Earth Ki

SHK elicits Heavenly Ki.

People's experiences of energies differ greatly, and what one person experiences can be very different from that experienced by other people carrying out the same exercise.

There is no 'right' way to experience the energies that CKR and SHK elicit.

Having said that, though, there is often a general trend, a similar theme that runs through people's descriptions of the energies elicited by these two symbols.

All I am looking for when you experience these energies is that, for you, there is some difference in the quality or characteristics or nature of the energies when you meditate on them.

You should also expect your experience of their energies to be fairly stable, in that when you meditate on them again, you should have some sort of a familiar experience in terms of how they affect you or the impression that you have of them, like coming back to a familiar friend: "oh, I recognise…"

On the next page you can see CKR and SHK, with instructions about how to draw them (what lines to draw in what order).

CKR

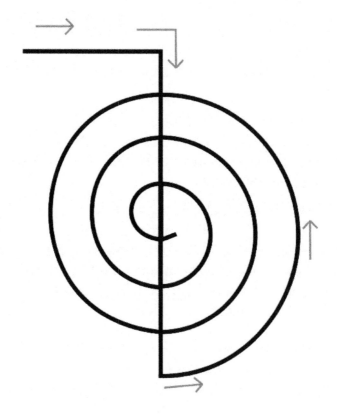

SHK

Symbol meditation focused on the Tanden

Here is a way of experiencing the energies of the symbols through meditation, and this should be carried out for 3-5 minutes for each symbol.

The meditation focuses on the Tanden, an energy centre located two fingerbreadths (3 – 5cm) below your tummy button and 1/3rd of the way into your body.

1. Sit comfortably with your eyes closed, with your hands resting in your lap and your palms facing upwards.
2. Visualise, say, SHK up in the air above you and say the symbol's name three times silently to yourself to 'empower' the symbol.
3. As you breathe in, draw energy down from the symbol. The energy passes through your crown, down the centre of your body to your Tanden.
4. As you pause before exhaling, feel the energy getting stronger in your Tanden.
5. As you exhale, flood the energy throughout your body.

You will have noticed that this exercise is a variation on Joshin Kokkyu Ho, but we have added the focus on a Reiki symbol. The symbol, imagined up in the air above you, represents the source of the energy, and doing this is a way of saying to yourself "I just want the energy of Earth Ki, say, to flow through me".

You visualise the symbol at the beginning of the exercise and you do not need to keep the symbol clear in your mind's eye for every second of the meditation.

Visualising with a definite intent at the start of the exercise is sufficient, though you may choose to renew the symbol by drawing it out again and saying its name to yourself three times again, at some stage during the meditation.

But do not go overboard with repeating the symbol as you meditate: this is unnecessary.

How do you feel? What sensations or impressions are you getting? How does the energy affect you in terms of your physical sensations and impressions, your mental state, your mental activity, your emotions?

Meditate on each symbol for a week and record your impressions on the pages below.

CKR meditations: what did you experience?

SHK meditations: what did you experience?

Why the Tanden?

The energy exercise above focused on an area of your body called the "Tanden" ("Dantien" or "Tan T'ien" in Chinese), an energy centre located two fingerbreadths (3 – 5cm) below your tummy button and 1/3rd of the way into your body.

You imagined that you were drawing energy – or light – into the Tanden and then moving the energy on elsewhere.

The Tanden point is seen as the centre of ourselves from the Oriental point of view, a seat of power, the centre of our intuitive faculties, the centre of life.

Drawing energy into your Tanden is drawing energy into the centre of your life and soul.

This area acts as a power centre that allows the amazing feats of martial artists to be performed, but also acts as the source of inspiration in Oriental flower arranging and calligraphy.

Meditation, exercise techniques like Tai Chi and Qi Gong, martial arts and Usui Reiki can all develop the Tanden.

The Tanden is thus seen as your personal energy store, the focus of your personal power. In energy cultivation techniques like Tai Chi and Qi Gong, the Tanden is the place where you store the energy that you are cultivating.

Conversely, a martial artist might draw down energy from the sun to store in their Tanden before moving on to spar with an opponent.

The Tanden is also regarded as the centre of your intuition and your creativity, so when people carry out Japanese calligraphy, or Ikebana (flower arranging) or the Tea Ceremony, they are focusing their attention on the Tanden, the centre of their being.

Basic Shapes to Explore

OK, so, having spent some time experiencing the energies of Earth Ki and Heavenly Ki by using the CKR and SHK symbols (which you may have been "attuned" to if you have attended a more standard Reiki Second Degree course), now we are going to move on to give you the opportunity to experience some different energies.

You will be accessing these energies by using symbols that you most certainly will not have been attuned to!

We will use simple symbols: a circle, a triangle and a square.

This may surprise you but these different geometrical shapes elicit quite different energies.

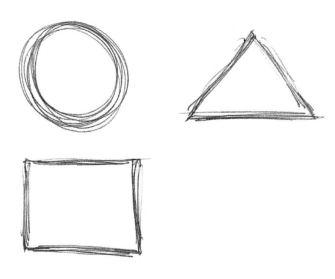

How to meditate on these shapes

Here is an alternative symbol meditation, which does not focus on the Tanden. You can use this instead of the meditation focused on the Tanden if you like.

Like before, the meditation can be carried for 3-5 minutes for each symbol:

1. Sit comfortably with your eyes closed, with your hands resting in your lap and your palms facing upwards.
2. Visualise the symbol up in the air above you
3. Imagine cascades of energy flooding down onto you from the symbol. The energy radiates onto your face, your torso and into your hands, flooding over you and flowing through your whole body. The energy surrounds and engulfs you.

How do you feel? What sensations or impressions are you getting? How does the energy affect you in terms of your physical sensations and impressions, your mental state, your mental activity, your emotions?

Make notes on what you experience for the three symbols on the pages that follow.

Do this for a week and, each time you meditate on the shape, add words that refine or add to your existing descriptions.

Make notes below on what you experienced, what impressions you had of this energy.

Make notes below on what you experienced, what impressions you had of this energy.

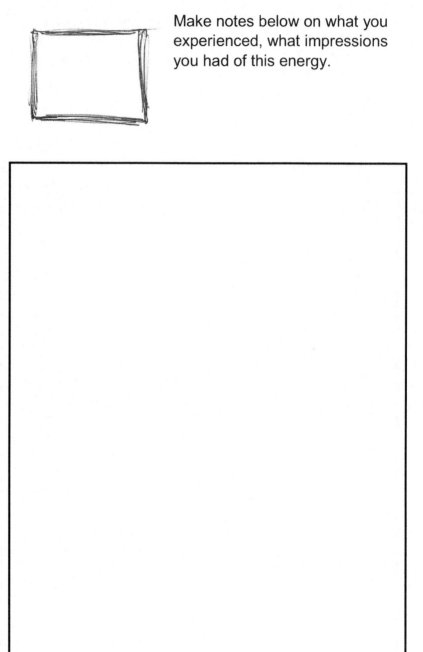

Make notes below on what you experienced, what impressions you had of this energy.

What Taggart noticed when meditating on these shapes

I spent some time meditating on these three shapes, experiencing their energies, and I planned to write down just three words that came to mind when experiencing them.

But additional words started coming to me, and that seemed to be useful, a way of rounding out the descriptions, so I kept going, and you can read what I experienced below.

WARNING:

I do not want you to play symbol "Bingo!" where you clench your fist and shout "YES!!" if you have written down the same word or words that I did.

My experience of these symbols in terms of how they felt and what impressions I received from them is not the definitive experience that you should be comparing yourself to or aiming to have experienced.

Your experience is your experience and that experience is valid. There are no correct or incorrect answers here.

What I am looking for is that, for you, there is some difference in the impression or impressions that you are receiving from these different symbols.

So having said that, this is what I noticed when experiencing the energies of these three symbols.

What Taggart noticed

	Solid, heavy, grounding, still, centred, physicality, earth, complete
	Uplifting, expansive, focused, mental acuity, competent, confident, at peace, enough, balance
	Powerful, emptiness, solidity, centred, nothing, balanced, nurtured, timeless

Practise More to Deepen Your Energy Sensitivity

So you practised experiencing the energies that were elicited by focusing on three shapes: a circle, a triangle and a square. If you would like to explore your energy sensitivity further and see what is possible for you, I have a further collection of shapes for you.

Take a look:

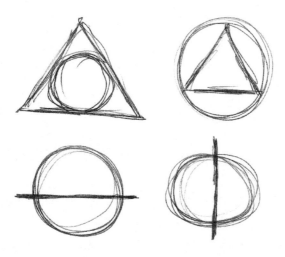

Now, you already know how to meditate on the energy of a novel symbol, so meditate on these and make notes on what feelings, thoughts or impressions you have.

How do you feel? What sensations or impressions are you getting? How does the energy affect you in terms of your physical sensations and impressions, your mental state, your mental activity, your emotions?

Make notes on what you experience for the four symbols on the pages that follow.

Do this for a week and, each time you meditate on the shape, add words that refine or add to your existing descriptions.

Make notes below on what you experienced, what impressions you had of this energy.

 Make notes below on what you experienced, what impressions you had of this energy.

Make notes below on what you experienced, what impressions you had of this energy.

Make notes below on what you experienced, what impressions you had of this energy.

What Taggart noticed when meditating on these shapes

Below you can see what impressions I had when working with these shapes and, again, please remember that my comments are not the 'correct' or definitive impressions that you need to compare your answers to.

There are no right or wrong answers here and your experience is your experience.

What I am looking for is that, for you, there is some difference in the impression or impressions that you are receiving from these different symbols.

	Movement, searching, flowing, gentle, delicate, precise

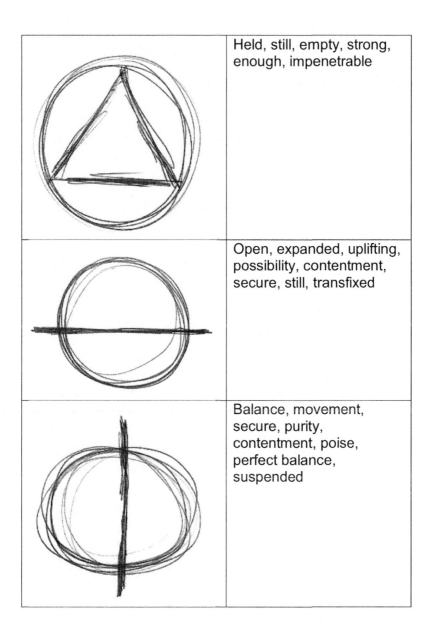

	Held, still, empty, strong, enough, impenetrable
	Open, expanded, uplifting, possibility, contentment, secure, still, transfixed
	Balance, movement, secure, purity, contentment, poise, perfect balance, suspended

A novel symbol for you to experiment with

Here is a further symbol for you, another combination of a circle and a square. Experiment with this: how is its energy different from the energies that you have experienced so far? Write your experiences below.

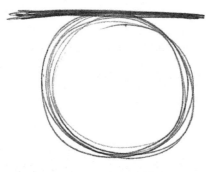

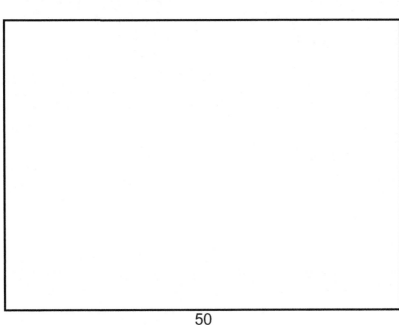

Energo-psychograms

In 2003 I was working with a lovely man in Moldova, Benedict Caraush. I was teaching him the Original Japanese Reiki methods and taking him through a distance Reiki Master Teacher course, and he was practising Reiju empowerments on his group of Reiki Master Teacher students.

One of his students had a special ability, a way of representing in graphic form the essence of an energy or an initiation. This is what Benedict said at that time:

> "One of this people have the ability to channeling the information on the paper like a drawing – energopsychograma. Some time ago she made for me the energopsychograms for how works Reiki on 1st, 2nd and 3rd degrees when people are attuned Western style (Takata). Next week I hope that she will be able to do the same work for the Reiju for 1st, 2nd and 3rd degrees in order to compare. If you are interested to see it, just let me know and I can scan it when will have it ready and send to you."

Benedict kindly shared with me a whole series of images detailing different energies and they are not available anywhere else.

As you will see below, an energopsychogram is not so much an image as a graphical representation or picture/drawing, but it still represents an energy and you can use the image to experience or elicit that energy, by meditating on it.

Obviously, you haven't been attuned to these!

How to meditate on Energopsychograms

To meditate on an energopsychogram, just sit calmly with the image in front of you. Stare at the image. let it wash over you, defocus your eyes.

Notice the quality of the energy that is being elicited within you. What is the nature of the energy? Where do you feel it? How does it feel? Bathe in the energy of the image.

Below you can find three energopsychograms relating to the energies of CKR and SHK, and to the state elicited by HSZSN, the distant healing symbol. See how you get on.

And if you would like to explore energopsychograms further, take a look at a series of blog posts I wrote about them, starting here. Scan this QR code:

Energopsychogram for CKR

Energopsychogram for SHK

Energopsychogram for HSZSN

Creating Bespoke Symbols

Hopefully you are now convinced and happy that you are able to experience the energy that comes from focusing on a variety of traditional and non-traditional symbols and images and that you do not need to have been 'attuned' to such a symbol or image for it to work for you.

Because now you are going to be creating your own bespoke symbols and use them for your own benefit, to help other people, and also to achieve particular purposes or enhance or emphasise a particular state or feeling.

But why do we even need symbols?

Before we move on to learn how to do this, there is a question about the use of symbols that needs to be addressed first.

The question is this: "If Reiki is intelligent and knows where to go and what to do, why do we need symbols?"

Well, we don't 'need' symbols, in that they are not an essential part of Reiki practice, but they are useful because they allow us to frame the energy in a certain way, narrowing the focus of the energy and in doing so increasing the power or intensity of what we are doing, rather like focusing a magnifying glass or a laser beam.

So, for example, by using CKR we emphasise Earth Ki and boost the flow of energy, or by using one of

Taggart's "Five Element Reiki" symbols we focus the energy intensely on the Wood element, or Water, narrowing the focus of the energy but making things more intense.

And if we are working intuitively when we treat someone, say – letting the energy or the recipient guide us in terms of which symbol we might use rather than trying to plan and 'work out' what might be best to use – then we are working in partnership with the energy, with the energy guiding us or helping us to understand what to focus our attention on or emphasise during the treatment.

Ask three questions to elicit a symbol

To create a symbol that will frame the energy in a way that perfectly matches your needs or the needs of your client, you can use these three questions, which you ask yourself:

1. If the energy that I need in this moment had a shape, what shape would it be?
2. If it had a colour, what colour would it be?
3. If that energy was to be held in a particular part of my body, where would it be held?

Allow the answers to come to you; go with the first thing that comes into your mind.

Write what came to you, or draw the symbol, or both:

So now you have, say, a green star that needs to reside in your abdomen (I have chosen this randomly).

To meditate on that symbol, imagine that shape in that colour, up in the air above you, representing the source of the energy. This is just like the symbol meditations that you were introduced to on the Reiki Evolution Second Degree course.

Imagine energy of that colour flooding down to you from the symbol above you, focusing/drawing the energy into that part of your body (in this example, the abdomen). Feel the energy in that location and allow that colour to flood through your whole body.

Experience that energy for a few minutes.

You could, of you like, imagine that the coloured symbol is actually passing into that location in your body, as that coloured energy continues to flow down to you from that symbol above you.

If you're not so good at visualizing at the moment, focus not so much on the shape of the symbol, but the feel of it, its texture or density: feel the shape rather than seeing it. If you can't see the colour very well, simply intend or 'know' that the shape and the energy has that particular hue.

In doing so, you are embodying the essence of that energy.

As a variation, you might draw the energy to your Tanden as you inhale, breathing the energy to its chosen location on the out-breath; experiment and find out what works best for you.

Ask the questions, and note what the symbol/colour etc. was, each day for seven days, and note your answers here:

Using the three questions with a client

To use this approach when treating someone, just slightly alter the three questions:

1. If the energy that they need in this moment had a shape, what shape would it be?
2. If it had a colour, what colour would it be?
3. If that energy was to be held in a particular part of their body, where would it be held?

Draw the coloured energy from that symbol above you, merge with the energy, and channel that colour energy to that part of their body using your hands/intent.

Creating Symbols for Particular Purposes

In the previous example we asked for "the energy that I need in this moment", but we can frame our question in a different way, to elicit an energy that provides us with the essence of a particular state or quality.

Maybe you might want to embody one of these states:

- Self confidence
- Serenity
- Relaxation
- Peaceful mind
- No mind
- Stillness
- Determination
- Compassion
- Motivation
- Creativity
- Contentment
- Enhanced intuition
- Rejuvenation

What useful or helpful states or qualities could you add to this list? Write them below.

What to ask to elicit the energy for yourself

To elicit such an energy for yourself, just modify the three questions a little, and meditate on or channel the energy (in this example, eliciting creativity):

1. If the energy of creativity had a shape, what shape would it be?
2. If it had a colour, what colour would it be?
3. If that energy was to be held in a particular part of my body, where would it be held?

Meditating on the energy

Imagine that shape in that colour, up in the air above you, representing the energy. This is just like the symbol meditations that you were introduced to on the Reiki Evolution Second Degree course.

Imagine that colour energy flooding down to you from above, focusing and concentrating itself in that part of your body. Feel the energy there and allow that colour to flood your whole body.

Experience that for a few minutes.

Alternatively, imagine that the shape moves down and resides in that part of your body, while coloured energy continues to flow down to that area from the symbol above you.

Use the meditation each day for a week and notice the difference within you.

Using a photographic image instead of a shape

Some people find that instead of a symbol, they have another image come to mind.

For example, stillness might be represented for you by the image of a still lake.

If that works for you then go with that, drawing energy from that image in whatever colour, if any, and to whatever location you are drawn to.

What to ask to elicit the energy for another person

To elicit such an energy for another person, use these questions and meditate on or channel the energy into the recipient:

1. If the energy of creativity *for this person* had a shape, what shape would it be?
2. If it had a colour, what colour would it be?
3. If that energy was to be held in a particular part of their body, where would it be held?

Allow the answers to come to you; go with the first thing that comes into your mind. So now you have, say, a yellow 2D disc that needs to reside in the client's solar plexus (I have chosen this randomly).

Channelling the energy for someone else

Imagine that shape in that colour, up in the air above you, representing the energy, as you might when using, say, CKR or SHK to treat someone.

Imagine that colour energy flooding down to you from above, flowing through you into the recipient; you focus your attention on that part of their body and imagine the energy/colour/symbol focusing and concentrating itself there.

You might have your hands resting on their shoulders, or you might choose to rest your hands on or near to the part of the body where the energy wants to reside; go with what feels right for you.

About the Author

Taggart King is a Reiki Master Teacher, Cognitive Hypnotherapist and NLP Master Practitioner who has been teaching Japanese-style Reiki through live and then home study courses for over 20 years.

He founded Reiki Evolution in 1998.

Taggart has written eight books about Reiki, created several Reiki-related journals and recorded a dozen audio collections (on CD and MP3) comprising guided meditations and audio commentary to accompany all the Reiki levels and practices.

Reiki Evolution

Reiki Evolution offers small-scale Reiki courses through a team of trusted teachers in the UK, all of whom offer Taggart's style of Reiki courses. There are never more than 4-6 students on any course so we can give you individual attention.

And finally, Taggart teaches Reiki mainly through home study courses.

Cognitive Hypnotherapy

Taggart qualified as a Cognitive Hypnotherapist in 2010, and as a NLP Master Practitioner with The Quest Institute, having trained with its founder, Trevor Silvester.

Taggart has also assisted in the training of new students on the Quest Diploma and NLP Master Practitioner courses.

Printed in Great Britain
by Amazon

38211582R00040